■ SCHOLASTIC

Cursive Writing Practice
Jokes & Riddles

40+ Reproducible Practice Pages
That Motivate Kids to Improve Their Cursive Writing

Violet Findley

New York • Toronto • London • Auckland • Sydney
Mexico City • New Delhi • Hong Kong • Buenos Aires

Teaching
Resources

Contents

Cover and interior design by Maria Lilja
Illustrations by Doug Jones

ISBN-13: 978-0-545-22752-0

Introduction

Welcome to *Cursive Writing Practice: Jokes & Riddles*! In the hustle and bustle of a hectic school day, cursive writing often gets short shrift. With reading, writing, math, science, and social studies to learn, few students have the time or inclination to perfect the fine art of the loop-the-loop. What a shame! Clear cursive writing is one of the best tools available to kids for efficient note taking and self-expression.

That's where these lively practice pages come in! In as little as five minutes a day, you can spur students to spruce up their cursive writing. Just reproduce and pass out a page, then sit back and watch kids move their pencils with levity and care. Why? Because the simple act of rewriting an amusing joke or riddle motivates them to master the shape, size, spacing, slant, and curve of model script.

And here's more good news: The completed practice pages can be quickly bound into instant joke-and-riddle books to share with family and friends. Can you think of a cooler way to showcase a child's carefully crafted script? I can't.

Read on to discover more tips for using this resource to improve your students' cursive writing and, in so doing, their essential communication skills.

Your partner in education,

Violet Findley

Using This Resource

This book has been designed for easy use. Before embarking on the joke and riddle pages, it's a good idea to review the basics. Do so by distributing the upper- and lowercase practice pages to students. These sheets include arrows showing the standard way to form each letter in cursive. As students complete these pages, circulate around the room looking for writing "red flags"—that is, kids who are forming their letters in nonstandard ways. If you notice an error, approach the student and model standard formation. This will help students rewire their cursive writing habits, which will improve both the clarity and speed of their printing down the road.

Once students have reviewed the basics, they're ready to enjoy the joke and riddle pages. These pages can be reproduced in any sequence you choose. Here are some simple routines for sharing them:

Cursive Writing Starters Place a practice page on each student's desk to complete first thing in the morning.

Cursive Writing Center Stock a table with a "practice page of the day" for students to complete independently.

Cursive Writing Homework Send home a page each night for students to complete in addition to the rest of their homework.

Cursive Writing Folders Create personal cursive writing folders filled with photocopies of the pages for students to complete at their own pace.

Meeting the 2–5 Language Arts Standards

Standard 3. Uses grammatical and mechanical conventions in written compositions

• Writes in Cursive

Source: *Content Knowledge: A Compendium of Standards and Benchmarks for PreK–12 Education* (4th Edition) (Mid-Continent Regional Educational Laboratory, 2004)

Making a Joke & Riddle Booklet

Once students have completed their pages, they can follow these simple directions to make personal booklets. Note: The booklets can comprise as many pages as you like. They need not include every page.

1. Cut the pages along the dashed lines, discarding the top portions.

2. Optional: Photocopy the blank booklet sheet on page 47 to add original jokes and riddles to the booklet.

3. Photocopy the booklet cover on page 48.

4. Place the booklet cover on top of the stacked pages in any order you choose.

5. Staple the book along the left-hand side.

6. Color the booklet covers and interior pages.

7. Share the booklet with family and friends.

Name _____

A B C D E
F G H I J K L M
N O P Q R S
T U V W X Y Z

Tip! Use the arrows to guide you in forming each letter.

Bonus Chuckle!

What's an eight-letter word that has only one letter in it?

An envelope!

Use your best cursive writing to copy each letter below.

A B C D E F G H I J K L M
N O P Q R S T U V W X Y Z
A B C D E F G H I J K L M N O P
Q R S T U V W X Y Z
A B C D E F G H I J K L M N O P
Q R S T U V W X Y Z
A B C D E F G H I J K L M N
O P Q R S T U V W X Y Z

Tip! Use the arrows to guide you in forming each letter.

Name _____

a b c d e f g h i j k l m
n o p q r s t u v w x y z

Use your best cursive writing to copy each letter below.

a b c d e f g h i j k l m n o p q r
s t u v w x y z a b c d e f g h i j
k l m n o p q r s t u v w x y z a
b c d e f g h i j k l m n o p

Cursive Writing Practice: Jokes & Riddles • © 2010 Scholastic • 6

Bonus Chuckle!

What word is always spelled incorrectly?

"Incorrectly"!

Dictionary

Name _____

Use your best cursive writing to copy the words.

boy boy boy boy boy boy boy

homework homework homework

teacher teacher

Use your best cursive writing to copy the sentences below.

Why did the boy eat up all of his homework?

Because his teacher said it was a piece of cake!

Tip: Check your SIZE. Is each of your letters the right height and resting neatly on the line?

Ha! • Ha! • Ha! • Ha! • Ha! • Ha!

Why did the boy eat up all of his

homework? Because his teacher said it

was a piece of cake!

Bonus Chuckle!

What school supply is always sleepy?

A nap-sack!

Tip! Check your SLANT. Do all your letters slant in the same direction?

Name _____

Use your best cursive writing to copy the words.

Cinderella Cinderella Cinderella

soccer soccer

pumpkin pumpkin

Use your best cursive writing to copy the sentences below.

Why did Cinderella lose every single soccer game? Because her coach was just a pumpkin!

Ha! • Ha! • Ha! • Ha! • Ha! • Ha!

Why did Cinderella lose every single soccer game? Because her coach was just a pumpkin!

Bonus Chuckle!

What did Cinderella say when her photos didn't arrive?

"Someday my prints will come!"

Name _____

Use your best cursive writing to copy the words.

white

black

zebra

Use your best cursive writing to copy the sentences below.

What is black and white and spins around?

A zebra stuck in a revolving door!

Tip! Check your SHAPE. Are all of your letters the right shape and closed where they should be?

Ha! • Ha! • Ha! • Ha! • Ha! • Ha!

What is black and white and spins around? A

zebra stuck in a revolving door.

Bonus Chuckle!

Why can't elephants ever get rich?

Because they work for peanuts!

Name _____

Use your best cursive writing to copy the words.

computer computer

squeak

mouse

Use your best cursive writing to copy the sentences below.

Why did the computer squeak? Because someone accidentally stepped on its mouse!

Tip! Check your SPACING. Are all of your letters and words evenly spaced?

SQUEAK!

Ha! • Ha! • Ha! • Ha! • Ha! • Ha! • Ha!

Bonus chuckle!

What did the baby computer call his father?

Data!

Name _____

Use your best cursive writing to copy the words.

monster *monster*

werewolf *werewolf*

mummy *mummy* *mummy*

Use your best cursive writing to copy the sentences below.

*What should you do if you find yourself in a room with
a monster, werewolf, and mummy? Stop imagining!*

Tip!
Check your
SMOOTHNESS.
Do all of your
letters have
the same line
thickness?

Ha! Ha! Ha! Ha! Ha! Ha!

What should you do if yourself in a

room with a monster, werewolf, and mummy?

Stop imagining.

Bonus chuckle!

What do you
call a very smart
monster?

Frank Einstein!

Name _____

Use your best cursive writing to copy the words.

Tarzan

golf

swing

Use your best cursive writing to copy the sentences below.

Why did Tarzan spend so much time on the golf

course? He wanted to improve his swing!

Ha! • Ha! • Ha! • Ha! • Ha! • Ha!

Tip! Clear your desk so you have room to write.

Bonus chuckle!

Why did the golfer bring an extra pair of pants?

In case he got a hole in one!

Name _____

Use your best cursive writing to copy the words.

math _math_

book _book_

problems _problems_

Use your best cursive writing to copy the sentences below.

Why was the math book always so unhappy?

Because it had lots and lots of problems!

Cursive Writing Practice: Jokes & Riddles • © 2010 Scholastic • 13

Tip! If you have to break a word at the end of the line, use a hyphen.

14+8=
12−5=

Ha! Ha! Ha! Ha! Ha! Ha!

Why was the math book always so unhappy? Because it had lots of problems.

Bonus Chuckle!

Why was six afraid of seven?

Because seven eight nine!

Use your best cursive writing to copy the words.

windows

ceiling

mushroom

Use your best cursive writing to copy the sentences below.

What room has no walls, no windows, no ceiling, no floor, and no door? A mushroom!

Tip! Practice your cursive writing a little each day.

Ha! • Ha! • Ha! • Ha! • Ha! • Ha!

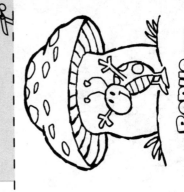

Bonus Chuckle!

What stays in the corner, but goes all around the world?

A stamp!

Name _____

Use your best cursive writing to copy the words.

cat

yarn

mittens

Use your best cursive writing to copy the sentences below.

Did you hear what happened to the female cat that
ate a big ball of yarn? She had a litter of mittens!

Tip! For extra practice, copy your favorite quotes in cursive.

Ha! • Ha! • Ha! • Ha! • Ha! • Ha!

Did you hear what happened to the female

Bonus chuckle!

Why are cats good at video games?

Because they have nine lives!

Practice Page
10

Tip! Always take your time and do your best.

Name _____

Use your best cursive writing to copy the words.

cross

jeans

encyclopedia

Use your best cursive writing to copy the sentences below.

What do you get when you cross a pair of blue jeans with an encyclopedia? A real smarty pants!

Ha! • Ha! • Ha! • Ha! • Ha! • Ha! • Ha!

Bonus Chuckle!

Where can a person always find money when they are looking for it?

The dictionary!

Name

Use your best cursive writing to copy the words.

cities

rivers

map

Use your best cursive writing to copy the sentences below.

What has cities without houses, roads without cars, rivers

without water, and forests without trees? A map!

Tip! Check your SIZE. Is each of your letters the right height and resting neatly on the line?

Ha! • Ha! • Ha! • Ha! • Ha! • Ha! • Ha!

Bonus Chuckle!

What did one map say to the other map?

Atlas we are together!

Name _____

Practice Page 12

Use your best cursive writing to copy the words.

strawberry

rutabaga

fight

Use your best cursive writing to copy the sentences below.

What do you call it when you see a strawberry punch a rutabaga? A food fight!

Tip! Check your SLANT. Do all your letters slant in the same direction?

Bonus Chuckle!

What is the funniest kind of soda?

Joke-a-cola!

Ha! Ha! Ha! Ha! Ha! Ha!

Name _____

Use your best cursive writing to copy the words.

President

standing

Because

Use your best cursive writing to copy the sentences below.

Why did President George Washington always sleep standing up? Because he could never lie!

Tip! Check your SHAPE. Are all of your letters the right shape and closed where they should be?

Ha! • Ha! • Ha! • Ha! • Ha! • Ha! • Ha!

Bonus chuckle!

What do you call a gorilla in a top hat?

Ape-aham Lincoln!

Name _____

Use your best cursive writing to copy the words.

centipede

school

brother

Tip! Check your SPACING. Are all of your letters and words evenly spaced?

Use your best cursive writing to copy the sentences below.

Why was the centipede late for school? Because he was playing "this little piggy" with his baby brother.

Ha! • *Ha!* • *Ha!* • *Ha!* • *Ha!* • *Ha!* • *Ha!* • *Ha!*

Bonus Chuckle!

What's worse than an alligator with a toothache?

A centipede with athlete's foot!

Name

Use your best cursive writing to copy the words.

giraffe

hedgehog

toothbrush

Use your best cursive writing to copy the sentences below.

What do you get when you cross a giraffe with a hedgehog? An extremely tall toothbrush!

Practice Page
15

Tip!
Check your
SMOOTHNESS.
Do all of your
letters have
the same line
thickness?

Ha! Ha! Ha! Ha! Ha! Ha! Ha! Ha!

Ha! • Ha! • Ha! • Ha! • Ha! • Ha!

Bonus chuckle!

What insect should never enter the boy's bathroom?

A lady bug!

Practice Page

16

Tip! Clear your desk so you have room to write.

Name _____

Use your best cursive writing to copy the words.

climb

rocket

space

Use your best cursive writing to copy the sentences below.

Why did Mickey Mouse climb inside a rocket and

blast off into outer space? He wanted to find Pluto!

Ha! • Ha! • Ha! • Ha! • Ha! • Ha! • Ha! • Ha!

Bonus Chuckle!

What happens when Donald Duck flies upside down?

He quacks up!

Name _____

Use your best cursive writing to copy the words.

bacon

toast

egg

Use your best cursive writing to copy the sentences below.

Why did the bacon and toast begin to laugh?

Because the egg cracked an excellent yolk!

Tip! If you have to break a word at the end of the line, use a hyphen.

Ha! Ha! Ha! Ha! Ha! Ha! Ha! Ha!
Ha! Ha! Ha! Ha! Ha! Ha! Ha! Ha!

Bonus Chuckle!

What do you call cheese that does not belong to you?

Nacho cheese!

Name _____

Use your best cursive writing to copy the words.

favorite

brand

Fruit

Use your best cursive writing to copy the sentences below.

What was King Tut's favorite brand of

underwear? Fruit of the Tomb!

Tip! Practice your cursive writing a little each day.

Ha! Ha! Ha! Ha! Ha! Ha! Ha!

Bonus Chuckle!

What did King Tut say when he was scared?

I want my mummy!

Name

Use your best cursive writing to copy the words.

dinosaur

chicken

pecks

Use your best cursive writing to copy the sentences below.

What do you get when you cross a fierce dinosaur with a hungry chicken? A Tyrannosaurus pecks!

Tip! For extra practice, copy your favorite quotes in cursive.

Ha! • Ha! • Ha! • Ha! • Ha! • Ha! • Ha! • Ha! • Ha!

Bonus chuckle!

What's the best way to call a T rex?

Long distance!

Name _____

Use your best cursive writing to copy the words.

hippopotamus

car

them

Use your best cursive writing to copy the sentences below.

What's harder than getting a hippopotamus into a compact car? Getting two of them into a compact car!

Tip! Always take your time and do your best.

Ha! Ha! Ha! Ha! Ha! Ha!

Bonus chuckle!

Where did the hippo get his shot?

In the hippobottomus!

Name _____

Use your best cursive writing to copy the words.

teacher

bird

conference

Use your best cursive writing to copy the sentences below.

Why was the teacher carrying a big bag of bird seed? She was going to a parrot-teacher conference!

Ha! Ha! Ha! Ha! Ha! Ha!

BIRD SEED

Bonus Chuckle!

Why did the teacher go to the beach?

She wanted to test the water!

Name _____

Use your best cursive writing to copy the words.

Atlantic

Pacific

waved

Use your best cursive writing to copy the sentences below.

What did the Atlantic Ocean say to the Pacific Ocean? Nothing, they both just waved!

Tip! Check your SLANT. Do all your letters slant in the same direction?

Bonus chuckle!

What never gets wetter no matter how much it rains?

The sea!

Ha! Ha! Ha! Ha! Ha! Ha! Ha!

Name

Use your best cursive writing to copy the words.

teddy

bear

cake

Use your best cursive writing to copy the sentences below.

What did the teddy bear say when he was offered a

slice of cake? "No, thank you, I'm totally stuffed!"

Tip! Check your SHAPE. Are all of your letters the right shape and closed where they should be?

Ha! • Ha! • Ha! • Ha! • Ha! • Ha!

Bonus Chuckle!

How did the teddy keep his house cool?

He used a bear conditioner!

Practice Page 24

Name _____

Use your best cursive writing to copy the words.

space

alien

weeder

Use your best cursive writing to copy the sentences below.

What did the space alien say to the flower bed?

Take me to your weeder!

Tip! Check your SPACING. Are all of your letters and words evenly spaced?

Bonus Chuckle!

Why did the Martian get a ticket?

Because he forgot to put money in the parking meteor!

Name _____

Use your best cursive writing to copy the words.

lady

change

weather

Use your best cursive writing to copy the sentences below.

Why did the lady stand outside with her purse open? She

wanted to see if there was any change in the weather!

Tip!
Check your
SMOOTHNESS.
Do all of your
letters have
the same line
thickness?

Ha! • Ha! • Ha! • Ha! • Ha! • Ha!

Bonus Chuckle!

Why did the lady put lipstick on her forehead?

She need to make up her mind!

Tip! Clear your desk so you have room to write.

Name _____

Use your best cursive writing to copy the words.

flamingos

stand

would

Use your best cursive writing to copy the sentences below.

Why do flamingos lift one leg when they stand?

If they lifted both legs, they would fall down!

Ha! Ha! Ha! Ha! Ha! Ha!

Bonus Chuckle!

Where does a peacock go if it loses its tail?

A re-tail store!

Tip! If you have to break a word at the end of the line, use a hyphen.

Name _____

Use your best cursive writing to copy the words.

octopus

hold

hand

Use your best cursive writing to copy the sentences below.

What did the boy octopus say to the girl octopus? I wanna

hold your hand, hand, hand, hand, hand, hand, hand!

Ha! • Ha! • Ha! • Ha! • Ha! • Ha! • Ha!

Bonus chuckle!

What do you call a fish with no eyes?

Fsh!

Name _____

Use your best cursive writing to copy the words.

snowman

baby

crib

Use your best cursive writing to copy the sentences below.

What did the snowman and his wife hang over

their new baby's crib?   A snowmobile!

Tip! Practice your cursive writing a little each day.

Ha! Ha! Ha! Ha! Ha! Ha!

Ha! Ha! Ha! Ha! Ha! Ha!

Bonus Chuckle!

What do you call a snowman in the summer?

A puddle!

Practice Page
29

Tip! For extra practice, copy your favorite quotes in cursive.

Name

Use your best cursive writing to copy the words.

hen

cement

brick

Use your best cursive writing to copy the sentences below.

What do you get when you cross a hen with a cement mixer? A bricklayer!

Ha! Ha! Ha! Ha! Ha! Ha! Ha!

Bonus chuckle!

What did the duck say when he dropped his dish?

"I hope it did not quack!"

Practice Page
30

Tip! Always take your time and do your best.

Name _____

Use your best cursive writing to copy the words.

teacher

class

bright

Use your best cursive writing to copy the sentences below.

Why did the teacher wear a pair of sunglasses when she entered the classroom? Because the kids were all so bright!

Ha! • Ha! • Ha! • Ha! • Ha! • Ha!

Bonus chuckle!

Why did the boy bring a ladder to school?

To get into high school!!

Name _____

Use your best cursive writing to copy the words.

seven

letters

refrigerator

Use your best cursive writing to copy the sentences below.

What seven letters did the boy say when he

opened up the refrigerator? "O I C U R M T!"

Tip! Check your SIZE. Is each of your letters the right height and resting neatly on the line?

Ha! Ha! Ha! Ha! Ha! Ha! Ha!

Bonus chuckle!

What do you call a fly with no wings?

A walk!

Name _____

Use your best cursive writing to copy the words.

basketball

drools

dribbles

Use your best cursive writing to copy the sentences below.

What is the difference between a beagle and a basketball player? One drools and the other dribbles!

Tip! Check your SLANT. Do all your letters slant in the same direction?

Ha! • Ha! • Ha! • Ha! • Ha! • Ha!

Bonus chuckle!

What kind of cats like to go bowling?

Alley cats!

Tip! Check your SHAPE. Are all of your letters the right shape and closed where they should be?

Name _____

Use your best cursive writing to copy the words.

carrots

rabbits

glasses

Use your best cursive writing to copy the sentences below.

How do you know carrots are good for your eyes?

Because you never see rabbits wearing glasses!

Ha! • Ha! • Ha! • Ha! • Ha! • Ha! • Ha!

Bonus Chuckle!

What do you call a bear with no teeth?

A Gummy Bear!

Name _____

Use your best cursive writing to copy the words.

black

white

skunk

Use your best cursive writing to copy the sentences below.

What is black and white and red all over? A baby

skunk with a very bad case of diaper rash!

Cursive Writing Practice: Jokes & Riddles • © 2010 Scholastic • 40

Tip! Check your SPACING. Are all of your letters and words evenly spaced?

Bonus chuckle!

What did the little porcupine say to the cactus?

"Is that you, Mommy?"

Ha! • Ha! • Ha! • Ha! • Ha! • Ha!

Name _____

Use your best cursive writing to copy the words.

ball

team

around

Use your best cursive writing to copy the sentences below.

Why did the soccer ball decide to quit the team?

It was sick and tired of being kicked around!

Tip!
Check your
SMOOTHNESS.
Do all of your
letters have
the same line
thickness?

Ha! • Ha! • Ha! • Ha! • Ha! • Ha!

Bonus Chuckle!

What should never be eaten after it is served?

A tennis ball!

Name _____

Use your best cursive writing to copy the words.

eighteen

flies

baseball

Use your best cursive writing to copy the sentences below.

What has eighteen legs and loves to catch flies?

A baseball team!

Tip! Clear your desk so you have room to write.

Bonus Chuckle!

Why did the coach go to the bank?

He wanted to get his quarterback!

Ha! Ha! Ha! Ha! Ha! Ha! Ha!

Use your best cursive writing to copy the words.

green

leafy

Elvis

Use your best cursive writing to copy the sentences below.

What is green and leafy and likes to wriggle its

hips when it sings? Elvis Parsley!

Tip! If you have to break a word at the end of the line, use a hyphen.

Bonus Chuckle!

What's green and croons romantic songs?

Frog Sinatra!

Ha! • Ha! • Ha! • Ha! • Ha! • Ha!

Name

Use your best cursive writing to copy the words.

house

right

left

Use your best cursive writing to copy the sentences below.

If the red house is on the right and the blue house is on the left, where is the white house? In Washington, D.C., of course!

Tip! Practice your cursive writing a little each day.

Ha! • Ha! • Ha! • Ha! • Ha! • Ha! • Ha!

Bonus Chuckle!

What is the color of a burp?

Burple!

Name _____

Use your best cursive writing to copy the words.

skeleton

dance

body

Use your best cursive writing to copy the sentences below.

Why did the skeleton stay home from the dance?

Because he had no body to go with!

Tip! For extra practice, copy your favorite quotes in cursive.

Ha! • Ha! • Ha! • Ha! • Ha! • Ha! • Ha!

Bonus Chuckle!

What do monsters order at McDonalds?

French frights!

Tip! Always take your time and do your best.

Name _____

Use your best cursive writing to copy the words.

pencil

circles

point

Use your best cursive writing to copy the sentences below.

What did the pencil sharpener say to the pencil?

Stop going around in circles and get to the point!

Bonus chuckle!

What school supply is king of the classroom?

The ruler!

Ha! Ha! Ha! Ha! Ha! Ha!

Ha! Ha! Ha! Ha! Ha! Ha! Ha!

The witch and the black cat flew away
on the brown broom.

Ha! Ha! Ha! Ha! Ha! Ha! Ha!

Booklet Covers Photocopy this page and cut along the dashed lines to create two booklet covers.

Jokes & Riddles

With cursive writing by

Nikhil Rao

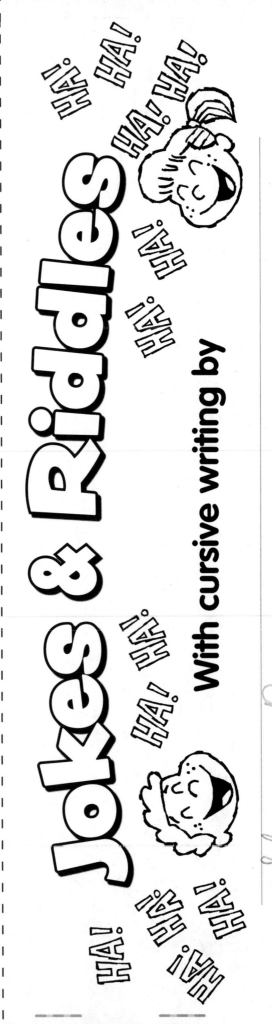

Jokes & Riddles

With cursive writing by

Shreya Rao